Grandma J

story by Lucy Floyd
illustrated by Mary Watson

HARCOURT BRACE & COMPANY

Orlando   Atlanta   Austin   Boston   San Francisco   Chicago   Dallas   New York
Toronto   London

All of the children on
Green Street love
Grandma J.
She isn't really their
grandma.
She is a special friend.

When Pete fell and hurt his knee, Grandma J made it better.

Kim liked to plant
flowers so Grandma J
showed her how.

Lee liked to draw pictures.
Grandma J always had
crayons.

When Maria really wanted a
pet, Grandma J found just
the right one.

The most special thing
about Grandma J was
the stories she told.

She told many stories
about living in Mexico and
her six older brothers,
who loved to spoil her.

"Now," Grandma J says, "I have my own children and grandchildren to spoil."

10

One day Kim went to
Grandma J's house, but no
one came to the door.
"Something is wrong,"
she said to Maria.
"Something is not right,"
said Lee.
"Where is Grandma J?"
asked Pete.

13

Someone had called 911 and help
came for Grandma J.
She had to rest her back.
But Pete made it better,
Kim brought flowers,
Lee drew pictures,
and Maria brought her pet.

And Grandma J told stories about living on Green Street and her four grandchildren who loved to spoil her.